THE MEDICAL MUSE

THE
MEDICAL MUSE

With a benign introduction by CHARLES W. MAYO, M.D.,

McGRAW-HILL BOOK COMPANY, INC.

or **What** *to* **Do** *Until the Patient Comes*
by RICHARD ARMOUR

and clinical exhibits by LEO HERSHFIELD

NEW YORK   TORONTO   LONDON

First Edition

Fourth Printing

02246

INTRODUCTION

"...Armour is his honest thought,
And simple truth his utmost skill."
—SIR HENRY WOTTON

Plato of Athens, who never was known to laugh very much, even in his youth, had a low opinion of poets. He thought that in the ideal republic all poets should be banished from the realm. This no doubt explains why he became well known for his ferocious scowl. Had he been exposed to some of the soaring wit and fancy of a well-tempered artificer like Richard Armour, he might have improved both his disposition and some of his gloomier pronouncements.

For what greater tribute can one man pay another than to say that in his contacts with his fellow man he possesses the rare ability to evoke a spontaneous smile up to and including a belly laugh, whether one reads aloud his sly poetry or prose in the standing, sitting, or prone position, enjoys it in the company of others who share in the fun, or absorbs it silently in any one of the above-named positions, alone in the quiet of a no-longer-lonely room.

This tribute I pay to Richard Armour, whose contributions to *Postgraduate Medicine* (to the unenlightened, the world's greatest medical journal, of which I am editor) have given the necessary light touch to an otherwise necessarily serious journal.

CHARLES W. MAYO, M.D.

THE MEDICAL MUSE

THE DOCTOR'S LIFE

Look up noses,
　Look down throats,
Look up nostrums,
　Jot down notes,

Look up rectums,
　Look down ears,
Look up patients
　In arrears,

Pull down covers,
　Pull up gowns. . . .
Life is full of
　Ups and downs.

GOOD CLEAN FUN

Give the hands a thorough scrubbing,
Lather well, and dry by rubbing,
Make a careful, close inspection,
Disinfect to foil infection.
Yet please think, while daubing, washing,
Of the germ you hope you're sloshing,
How this creature, strong but small,
Never takes a bath at all,
Never fools with germicide
On his dirty little hide,
Never washes either end
Lest he harm a little friend
Or, still graver, run the peril
Germs fear most, of being sterile.

URINALYSIS

Some bring their sample in a jar,
    Some bring it in a pot,
Some bring a sample hardly ample,
    While others bring a lot.

Some hide it in a paper bag,
    Some wrap it like a treasure,
Some, quite undaunted, proudly flaunt it
    As if it gives them pleasure.

Some cork it up so tightly that
    It's quite a job to spring it,
Some let it slosh, almost awash,
    And some forget to bring it.

NEW M.D.

The long, long learning years are past,
    He's feeling all a-tingle.
He has an office, has a nurse—
    There hangs his shiny shingle.
His waiting room is empty still,
    The magazines are tidy.
He opened up on Monday and,
    Well, here it is just Friday.
At last here's what he's craved for years,
    He's ready, now, for fees.
He has a private practice, yes—
    But not too private, please!

KNOWING THEIR PLACE

*There is a difference of opinion among British doctors
about where a man should be when his wife is having a
baby. One school of thought: right there with her in the
delivery room. The other: as far away as possible, prefer-
ably in the neighborhood pub.* —NEWS ITEM

A woman's place is in the home,
    Except when in delivery.
But where's her husband's, while he waits
    All jittery and quivery?

Some say his place is by her side,
    With rubber gloves and mask on,
To stand up close and peek and peer
    And urge the doctor's task on.

But others (no doubt fathers, these,
    Who speak with much authority)
Insist a pub's the place to be,
    And they're in the majority.

THE TONGUE DEPRESSOR

The tongue depressor does the trick
    On old as well as young.
The gadget's really rather slick
    For holding down the tongue.

Although it's somewhat short and flat,
    It's like a magic wand
For making tongues lie down so that
    The view is clear beyond.

The tongue depressor's useful for
    Maneuverings like these,
And yet the doctor's even more
    Depressed by what he sees.

WALK OF LIFE

*Walking is the best of all exercises, according
to medical studies.*   —NEWS ITEM

"Exercise," the doctor said,
    "I certainly suggest.
And studies in the field of med-
    Icine say walking's best.

"It helps the breathing, helps the heart,
    Improves the muscle tone.
And now excuse me, must depart."
    And he hung up the phone

And walked, yes walked and walked, it's true,
    With healthful stride. How far?
From where he had been sitting to
    His car.

WHEN DUTY CALLS

The obstetrician, roused from bed,
   Gets up all cold and shivery
And has to drive at breakneck speed
   To make a quick delivery.

The surgeon leaves his food untouched
   (The call is full of urgency)
And hastens to the hospital
   To meet a dire emergency.

And both of them, when torn from sleep
   Or when a meal is missed,
Ask, "Why did I not choose to be
   A dermatologist?"

10

JUST LOOK AT HIM

His jacket's white and newly starched,
His eyebrows with concern are arched,
His accent and mustache are clipped,
His hands are scoured, his nails are nipped.

His bedside manner is superb,
He never wastes a noun or verb,
He is the sort, well-poised and just,
That patients all respect and trust.

Where will you find, where will you see,
This model of what all should be?
Not in a school or clinic, no,
But on a weekly TV show.

MEDICAL MEETING

Hurrah for the medical meeting
   And learning whatever is new,
Along with some excellent eating
   And maybe some drinking too.

Hurrah for seeing new places
   And learning what's what and why,
And hundreds of fresh new faces,
   A joy to the jaded eye.

Hurrah for what's new in dissecting,
   And cures in which science now glories,
And best, hurrah for collecting
   A number of brand-new stories.

BURTON REVISITED,
OR THE MELANCHOLY OF ANATOMY

Many strain their back
And get out of whack
The sacroiliac.
They are down and through
For a while. And yet few

Have cause to complain
Of straining the brain.
This should make it plain
Brain and back, in most cases,
Ought to change places.

PICTURE THIS

Before and After pictures of
Patients, I admit I love.
The picture on the left displays
A person doomed in many ways,
With ghastly pustules, fearsome lesions,
With gangrene, tumors, and adhesions,
Obese, far gone with insobriety,
A mental case, due to anxiety.
Then on the right I see this very
Patient hale and sleek and merry,
Completely free of all his ills,
And gladly paying doctors' bills.
Oh, what a contrast, what improvement,
What gratifying forward movement.
All praise to science, let's agree—
The science of photography.

SURE CURE

By vinegar and honey, mixed,
Now almost every ailment's fixed:
Insomnia, skin rash, bronchitis,
Obesity, and hepatitis,
As well as colds and hypertension
And other ills that one might mention.

Yes, vinegar and honey solely
Will cure the ailing patient wholly.
It is the best of wonder drugs
With which to rout all sorts of bugs.
At least so says Aunt Sarah, who
Is quite convinced that this is true

Because she heard it from Miss Doakes,
A solemn sort, who never jokes,
Who heard it from a Mrs. Ide,
Who can't be interviewed. She died.

THE DRUGGIST

The druggist is the doctor's friend,
   He serves him with devotion.
For him his shelves and counters bend
   With every pill and potion.

The druggist works with all his might,
   He gets down early, Monday.
He toils away till late at night;
   His store is open Sunday.

The druggist's quite a pleasant man,
   His jokes are sometimes ribald.
And best, he reads (no other can)
   The words the doctor scribbled.

Consider those diseases
   The doctor daily treats:
The pains no potion eases,
   The heart that oddly beats,

The twinges that give omen
   Of troubles of the gland,
The ailments of abdomen,
   The tremors of the hand. . . .

Each ill at last is verified,
   He sees each patient through,
Then thinks (and is he terrified!)
   He has the symptoms, too.

RIGOROUS ROUTINE

The British Ministry of Health is concerned about the rigorous hospital routine that allows patients little opportunity for rest. —NEWS ITEM

In England and the U.S. too
A patient has so much to do—
With checks on fever, tongue-depressings,
Washings, changings, pills, and dressings,

Bedmakings, feedings, visitations,
Pulse-feelings, hypos, medications,
This-side-to-that-side frequent turning,
Exhibits to the young and learning—

That some who live through operations
And dread diseases and dilations
May, on the day discharged so freely,
Succumb—from sheer exhaustion really.

THE MALADJUSTED MOTHER

The maladjusted mother
  Is the pitifullest sight.
There is hardly any other
  In so horrible a plight.

There she leans, or sags, despondent
  On the ironing board at home,
Overeating fudge and fondant,
  Overpolishing the chrome,

And, a captive of compulsion,
  On the edge of cracking up,
She feels loathing and revulsion
  For her children and her pup.

Yes, we call her maladjusted—
  Term psychiatrists have scooped—
But she knows, and she's disgusted,
  That her feet hurt, and she's pooped.

THEIR BITE IS WORSE THAN THEIR BARK

Much more beset by dogs than most men,
Far more, indeed, than even postmen,
Are doctors who, although it rankles,
Have canines sniffing at their ankles
And dogging every rear and fore step
Between the gateway and the doorstep.
How best to manage? Soothe the critter
With calming words? Haul off and hit her?
Walk firmly on, the little distance,
Or stop and bellow for assistance?

A doctor, as he comes a-bounding,
Must take from hounds a lot of hounding,
And, called for heart attacks or babies,
Should take along some shots for rabies.

MUSCLING IN

A researcher says that muscles emit electric signals in a frequency range used by trans-Atlantic radio broadcasts.
—NEWS ITEM

Research again has breached the dyke,
    And we are all atwitter.
To think of muscles sending like
    A radio transmitter!

Pray tell us also, probing man,
    For nothing's past believing:
If muscles send out signals, can
    They also be receiving?

If so, I'll make my deltoids dance,
    And flex my biceps prettily,
And say hello to friends in France,
    In England, and in Italy.

CURE-IT-YOURSELF

Do-It-Yourself is the rage of the day,
Be it building a birdhouse or squirting a spray,
Undenting a fender or patching a tire,
Repairing a faucet or taping a wire.

And what if the craze—every man his own Edison—
Should spread from the home and the office to
                    medicine?
Yes, what if the patient, with pills on his shelf,
Should guess at his ailments, prescribe for himself,

And snip out his tonsils (he mirrors the view)
And, if he can manage, his hemorrhoids too?
The doctor may suffer, and so may the nurse,
But the do-it-yourselfer will suffer still
                    worse!

COLD COMFORT

*Scientists are called to redouble efforts
to end the common cold.* —NEWS ITEM

Isolate the virus,
    Investigate the mold.
Come, let this call inspire us
    To end the common cold.

And when the cold is ended
    From shore to distant shore,
Mankind will be befriended
    And noses run no more.

Full victory the achers
    And sneezers will achieve,
And only, then, the makers
    Of handkerchiefs will grieve.

23

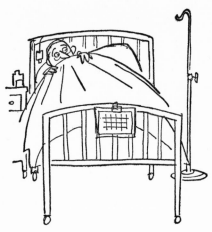

SHOCK TREATMENT

A study reveals that model patients are merely afraid of nurses.
                                                    —NEWS ITEM

How shattering, to learn that he
    Who did just as directed—
Took pills as if with greatest glee,
    Lay quiet while injected—

Was not, as thought, a person kind,
    Agreeable, and willing
(A sort you very rarely find,
    And when you do, it's thrilling),

But someone scared of nurses, friend,
    Who will perhaps, some night,
Though seeming surely on the mend
    Scream out, and die of fright.

HOSPITAL BEDS

Hospital beds, of steel and chrome,
Are higher than the ones at home,
And patients often pale with fright
On looking down from such a height.

Yes, they are dangerous to crawl from
And really damaging to fall from,
And it's no wonder patients peer
Down at the floor with wide-eyed fear.

But if these beds that so appall
Must really, truly be at all,
It's good, at least, that they are where
Those falling get the best of care.

WORDSWORTH REVISITED

A newly discovered drug, lycoramine, that is found in the bulbs of daffodils, may prove effective in the treatment of myasthenia gravis, a neuromuscular disease.

—AMERICAN DRUGGIST

I wandered lonely as a cloud
    Among the lovely hills,
And suddenly came on a crowd
    Of golden daffodils.

My heart leapt up when I beheld
    Those daffodils so gay.
I cried, as joy within me welled,
    "This is my lucky day!

"I shall uproot these flowers found,
    Though some may think me silly.
They'll bring at least a buck a pound
    From Squibb or Eli Lilly!"

UNFAIR TO SPIDERS

The derangement of spiders fed hallucinogenic drugs can be detected in the pattern of their webs. —NEWS ITEM

"Won't you come into my parlor?"
    Said the spider to the fly.
As it happened, this gay spider,
    Fed with drugs, was feeling high.

"Aw, come on," called out the spider,
    With a lurch and with a leer,
But the fly just kept his distance
    And, indeed, seemed not to hear.

For the web was oddly tangled,
    With a sag in one locality,
And the fly, a decent fellow,
    Was repelled by abnormality.

Thus it was, for sake of science,
    That the spider, though no sinner,
Made a pattern like a slattern
    And was cheated of his dinner.

HOLD EVERYTHING

Children wiggle,
   Children squirm.
Ever try to
   Hold a worm?

Children fidget
   While you work.
Just get set,
   And children jerk.

Offices,
   Though well equipped,
Need one thing,
   I say, tight-lipped:

Nothing else
   Would be so nice
Or so useful
   As a vise.

NOTE TO DERMATOLOGISTS

Long Island University scientists have discovered that perfume oils kill bacteria and fungi, both for the person who wears the perfume and the one who inhales it.

—NEWS ITEM

The perfume worn by Jane or Nancy
Does more than merely stir the fancy,
Does more, indeed, with its aroma,
Than leave men in a helpless coma.

Bacteria and fungi squirm
No longer on the epiderm
That's daubed or sprayed or doused quite well
With scents of Lanvin or Chanel.

So tell the somewhat worried male:
Go on and sniff the girl, inhale;
You'll get the thrill that you'd expected,
And, what is more, be disinfected.

DOCTORS' SCALES

Here's a curious thing about doctors' scales,
And something that rarely if ever fails:
To obese they weigh heavy, to thin they weigh light,
Which means that few patients consider them right.

They're excellent scales, surely better than many,
They cost, when you bought them, a pretty penny,
They satisfy those in professional sectors,
Like, well, like the state and the county inspectors.

But patients are skeptical, scenting a plot,
If they don't weigh enough or they do weigh a lot,
So they check up on scales that can really be trusted—
The ones in their bathroom that they have adjusted.

WHERE'S THE DOCTOR?

Is there a doctor in the house?
If you should ask a doctor's spouse,

The chances are, statistics show,
The answer you would get is, "No."

The doctor's at the office, working
 (It's after hours and rather irking),

Or on a call out in the sticks
Or at a meeting, just for kicks,

Or north of Rio, south of Nome,
But not, or very rarely, home.

A LITTLE LEARNING

Patients once let surgeons cut
Without an if or and or but.
They rarely raised demanding questions
And never offered up suggestions.

Patients once, not long ago,
Believed the doctor ought to know,
Submitted with the best of will,
And trusted in his practiced skill.

But patients now, and patients' wives,
Are sharper than a surgeon's knives,
And argue over each incision. . . .
They've seen it all on television.

SALES INSISTENCE

The pathways to the doctor's door,
　　The front and back as well,
Are trod by none so numerous
　　As those with things to sell.

Here come the salesmen tall and short,
　　The dark and also blond men,
Insurance, auto, real estate,
　　As well as stock-and-bond men.

Fair game for all, the doctor is,
　　His name on every list.
He needs a nifty practice or
　　A tough receptionist.

DOCTOR'S WIFE

I beat the drum, I blow the fife,
I bow before the doctor's wife.
Show me a woman any smarter,
More of a saint, more of a martyr,
More of a stoic sort than she
Who chose to marry an M.D.
She keeps the books, makes out the bills,
And holds her tongue on patients' ills.
She waits the dinner as she's told,
Then eats it by herself, and cold.
And mostly staying home alone
And answering the telephone,
She says the doctor (here's the prize)
Will soon be there—and knows she lies.

BEHOLD THE PATIENT

Behold the patient uncomplaining,
Not asking whether losing, gaining,
Not offering unsought advice,
But really being very nice.

Behold the patient (best of scenes)
Not tearing up the magazines,
Not pacing up and down the floor,
Not hammering upon the door.

Behold the patient quite relaxed,
With nerves, this once, not overtaxed,
Serene, almost unrecognized,
Not fighting back—anesthetized.

PHYSICIAN, STEEL THYSELF

Rittelmeyer urges the physician never to prescribe a restrictive diet unless he has first tried it himself.
   —JOURNAL OF THE AMERICAN MEDICAL ASSOCIATION

The notion here advanced of diet
   May have a wider scope.
Each medicine you give, first try it,
   And when you've tried it, hope.

An appendectomy? I beg
   You, take your own out first.
Don't amputate an arm or leg
   Till likewise you've rehearsed.

This way you'll gain in sympathy
   And human understanding,
Although your work may come to be
   Perhaps a bit demanding.

THE ANESTHETIST

Give heed to the anesthetist,
A person who'd be sorely missed
By patients who object to pain
And surgeons cutting limb or brain
And nurses who well earn their wages
By feeling pulses, watching gauges.
It's the anesthetist, no less,
Who's conscious of unconsciousness
And, checking closely, doles the gas out
Until the lucky patients pass out.

WISE GUY

Who knows each illness, knows each cure?
Who never doubts, is always sure?
Who gives advice to learned scholars
And shrugs aside their thanks and dollars?

Who is this awesome fellow, friends?
Who is the chap who condescends
To chat with men like Mayo? Who?
It is the intern, young and new,

Who knows more than all other men.
He'll never know so much again.

SOUND HEALTH?

Burps Held Clues to Ills of Patients.
—NEWSPAPER HEADLINE

It seems that now a way is found
To tape, and analyze, the sound
A patient makes who burps a bit
And, blushing, says, "Please pardon it."

A baby's burp may well be harmless,
But in adults it signals charmless
Diseases such as prostatitis,
Glaucoma, athlete's foot, arthritis,

Pneumonia, worms, tuberculosis,
Shingles, migraine, carcinosis,
And even, though there may be question,
In some rare cases indigestion.

SLAVE LABOR

Lucky doctor, I insist,
Who's had the same receptionist
For twenty years, day after day,
And never asked a raise in pay.

One who, moreover, keeps accounts
And watches even small amounts
As if the income she bestirs
Herself to guard, were partly hers.

But will this creature not be lured
To something better? Rest assured
She'll stay, if need be, all her life,
For she's the lucky doctor's wife.

ON CALL

Over the hospital speaker,
  Over and over and over,
Comes "Calling Dr. Delancey"
  Or "Calling Dr. McGrover,"

Or "Calling Dr. Padelford"
  Or "Drs. Schwartzkopf and Gill"
Or "Calling Dr. Bonelli"
  Or "Calling Dr. Cahill."

From morning till night for someone
  The squawkbox forever is squalling,
For medicine isn't a business,
  It is, very clearly, a calling.

SCHOOL PHOBIA

Children who experienced anxiety symptoms while refusing to go to school were treated at Houston State Psychiatric Institute, where it was found that tranquilizing drugs were effective in overcoming the school phobia. —NEWS ITEM

It used to be, when we were small,
    Without the least remorse
A truant officer would call
    And drag us off by force.

They didn't know that we were sick,
    In psychiatric trouble.
Our parents treated us, and quick,
    With whacks, while we bent double.

But now they recognize the ill,
    At least at quite a few spots,
And would-be truants take a pill
    And save some black-and-blue spots.

RASH REMARK

Consider the bothersome, ugly skin rash,
The crusty thick or the blushing thin rash.
It may be something the patient ate,
It may be caused by the patient's mate,
It may be nerves and it may be weather
 (For human skin isn't tough as leather),
It may be psychotic, or even prenatal,
But remember this: it is never fatal.

It may cause itching, it may look bad
And embarrass the hell out of some poor lad,
It may mean scratching a certain place
That's hard to get at, in public, with grace.
But here's the prognosis you've got to give:
"Whether you want to or not, you'll live."

SPLIT PERSONALITY

Fee splitting is a frightful thing,
   A dreadful thing to do.
Throughout the whole profession it
   Is said to be taboo.

And yet I must confess I know,
   Among the best M.D.s,
A doctor who goes right ahead
   And openly splits fees.

He doesn't like to do it, but
   He shrugs, says, "Well, that's life,"
And counting out the cash received,
   He splits fees—with his wife.

OH, RATS!

Studies at the University of Michigan show that when rats are taught to drink, early learners drink more than late learners, those with distressing problems drink more than others, and male rats drink more than females.

—NEWS ITEM

Since I have never cared for rats,
There is a job I'd like, and that's
The one of teaching rats to drink.
It would be rather fun, I think.

Ostensibly for science, I
Would love to get some rodents high,
And have them staggering about
And getting sick, and passing out.

And when I'd jotted notes, all clinical,
And rats were blotto, I, quite cynical,
Would leave the lab on stealthy toe
And summon in a cat I know.

45

SUNDAY

Sunday is, or so it's said,
A day for staying late in bed,
For letting whiskers grow and harden,
For cultivating home and garden,
For reading books, both gay and boresome,
For golfing with the good old foursome,
For eating snacks and sipping slowly,
Relaxing pleasantly and wholly.

And Sunday is of course the day
When patients have a fiendish way
Of getting fingers caught in mowers
And running head-on into doors
And getting beaned upon the links
And passing out from "poisoned" drinks
And keeping thus, with zeal and zest,
The doctor from his day of rest.

BREAKFAST SERIAL

Who's this, at the corner drugstore,
    A sallow, dyspeptic fool,
Who gulps down a hasty breakfast
    And breaks each nutritional rule?

Who's this, in a terrible hurry,
    What ignorant, uninformed rookie,
Whose regular breakfast's a cup
    Of coffee, topped off by a cookie?

Who is he? I sorrow to tell you
    The chap's a distinguished physician,
Sought out by a great many patients
    Because of his work in nutrition.

ANOTHER ONE

Another doctor's come to town,
  Hung out his hopeful shingle,
Bought office furnishings of chrome,
Paid down a payment on his home,
  Begun to mix and mingle.

Another doctor's come to town,
  And come, it seems, to stay.
And it has been a dozen years
Since any doctor, it appears,
  Has died or moved away.

Another doctor's come to town,
  His name is on the door,
And, strangely, though there was mistrust
At first, the doctors all are just
  As busy as before.

KIBITZERS

One thing about a house-call's this:
There's always someone, man or miss,
An uncle, sister, father, brother,
A cleaning woman, or some other,
Who hovers close with piercing questions
And admonitions and suggestions.

Sometimes a neighbor happens by
To lend a hand (and tongue and eye)
And tell, although she isn't bid,
The wondrous things her doctor did
And make you feel an awful fool
With need of going back to school.

A doctor merits extra salary
For working when he has a gallery.

CONVENTIONAL SITUATION

What doctor, however honest,
    However righteous and pure,
Doesn't plan for a three-day convention
    As part of a three-week tour?

Is the meeting in New York City?
    Well, wise as an ancient Buddha,
He goes or he comes by a routing
    That plops him awhile in Bermuda.

Is the meeting in San Francisco?
    Just study it closely and see—
There might be a sort of a circle
    With a stop-off in Waikiki.

Yes, doctors convene to hear speeches
    And papers by erudite chaps,
But what is that bulge in their pockets?
    Most likely it's tickets and maps.

THE WHEEL CHAIR

The wheel chair, when it's self-propelled,
Can go as if bat-out-of-helled,
And with no sound of motor humming
Gives you no warning that it's coming.

On rubber tires, with spinning spokes,
It sneaks up on unwary folks,
On doctors, nurses, friends and foes,
And bashes rears and crushes toes.

Oh, cars and trucks are fierce on highways,
And so are bicycles in byways,
But in a dimly lighted corridor
The swift and silent wheel chair's horrider.

HURRY CALL

They say it's an emergency,
   They beg of you, "Come quick!"
They stress the awful urgency,
   They say they're mighty sick.

They scream the vital message,
   They're almost out of breath.
Their symptoms seem to presage
   A very early death.

The streets are slick and wet there,
   And getting slicker, wetter. . . .
And when at last you get there,
   You find they're feeling better.

WANT TO HEAR SOMETHING FUNNY?

What makes a patient laugh and laugh,
    As soon as he is told?
It's hearing (he's incredulous)
    His doctor has a cold.

To think that he, with all he knows,
    With every sort of pill,
Should have the rank incompetence
    To let himself get ill!

The doctor, meanwhile, sees no joke,
    No smile is on his mug,
To hear the patient jest from whom
    He knows he got the bug.

BORN TOO SOON

Poor Grandfather lived in an ignorant age,
   At how little he knew, we recoil.
He never once read, not a chapter or page,
   Of the virtues of safflower oil.

He drank and he smoked, he ate animal fat
   As much as he could on his salary.
Cholesterol count? He knew nothing of that,
   And he never once counted a calorie.

Poor Grandfather's gone. At his head there's a stone.
   God rest him, in hell or in heaven.
He might still be living if only he'd known,
   But he died when but eighty-seven.

PROFESSIONAL CONDUCT

A doctor cannot advertise,
    It is the worst of vices.
He may well cut his patient but
    He mustn't cut his prices.

A doctor must not treat and tell
    In gossip or derision.
He must be very circumspect
    About a circumcision.

A doctor walks a narrow path,
    With many quick to shame him.
If now and then he has a fling,
    I really wouldn't blame him.

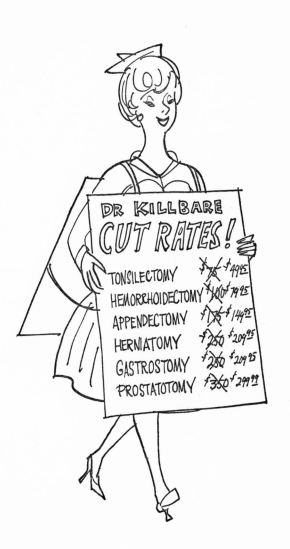

DOC ISN'T DOCTOR, IT'S
DESOXYCORTICOSTERONE

*Perhaps the time has come when we may have to develop
a set of shorthand symbols for medical topics, corresponding
to the notes of music and the symbols of algebra.*
   —JOURNAL OF THE AMERICAN MEDICAL ASSOCIATION

The time has come, the doctor said,
    To write of many things,
Nephrectomy, hypoxia,
    And aural openings.

In symbols, though, and not in words.
    It really will be ducky
When Ky stands for kidney, not
    For Kinsey or Kentucky.

Yes, A is acne, B is blood,
    And C is constipation.
And Hi? Well, it's histology,
    And not a salutation.

THE STETHOSCOPE

Come, hail the handy stethoscope
    Through which the doctor hears
The whirs and rasps and wheezy gasps
    That beat upon his ears.

The stethoscope's a nice device
    For picking up the sounds
Of sundry leaks and burps and squeaks
    And thuds and pops and pounds.

And best of all, like earphones, it's
    For private hearing merely.
The patient can't hear ping or pant,
    Although he'd love to, dearly.

PREDICTION

Doctors admit they cannot predict with accuracy the age when an infant will start sleeping through the night.
—NEWS ITEM

This will come as quite a shock
To those who count on Dr. Spock,
Will undermine the faith, as well,
Of those who swear by Doc Gesell.

Yes, even men with lofty domes
Who write authoritative tomes
Can't tell the parent (haggard, glum)
Just when the happy change will come.

But come it will, though not on charts,
When red are eyes and leaden hearts,
And once-despairing Dad and Mother
Will start to think, "Let's have another."

THE HYPOCHONDRIAC

This patient wails of troubles
   That don't, in fact, exist.
With fancied pain he doubles,
   Complaining of a cyst,
Or burns, he says, with fever,
   Though normal when you check.
This panting, paining griever
   Pains others in the neck.
Some day, should he be stricken
   For real, I'll understand
If he is left to sicken
   And no one lifts a hand.

CLINICAL NOTE ON BRAVERY

A very common theme of jokes,
   As well as of cartoons,
Is how, when hypo nears his hide,
   Some big strong fellow swoons.

The hairy-chested he-man type,
   The driver of a bus,
Faints dead away, sometimes, from fear,
   And makes a dreadful fuss.

Now this is very funny. Yes,
   And more than likely true,
Except that frail and skinny chaps
   Are thus affected, too.

CHRONIC CONDITION

Let's diagnose the patient who
Gets pains when doctors' bills are due,
Excruciating pains that stab
His shoulder when he starts to grab
Some cash from out his pocketbook.
Oh, doctor, what an anguished look,
And what a throbbing of the neck
If he should try to write a check.
It shows that there's congestion, tightening,
A state of shock that's truly frightening.

If such a sickness needs a name
To give it proper place and fame,
Here's one (if you've a better, write us):
Disbursitis.

TABOO OR NOT TABOO

The prostate gland is strangely, and unnecessarily, taboo in conversation.
—NEWS ITEM

Just listen to the ceaseless yak
Of him, the poor insomniac,
Or hear for hours the man with gout
Or chap who had a kidney out.

How tirelessly a man will speak
Of how he had a narrow squeak
From gallstones or from hypertension.
But prostate trouble? Not a mention.

If doctors only could convince
Their patients that they needn't wince
At whispers of the prostate gland,
Well, conversation *would* be grand!

SKIN GAME

I hail the dermatologist,
  Who works upon the skin.
His field is not so deep as wide,
He sees what's going on outside
  While others grope within.

    His patients walk, his patients drive,
      They're mostly mobile, very.
    And house calls paid to distant lanes
    To minister to aches and pains
      Are quite unnecessary.

        And best, at night he's not disturbed,
          No phone rings on the shelf.
        His blissful sleep's a sweet caress
        Between unrumpled sheets—unless
          He has an itch himself.

CASE IN POINT

The case was very strange indeed,
   He couldn't diagnose it.
He couldn't seem to get a lead
   Or figure how to dose it.

And yet it seemed familiar too,
   As if encountered previous.
He thought he had at last a clue,
   Though faint, as yet, and devious.

An article! Yes, that was right
   (The patient meanwhile bleeding),
An article he never quite
   Had got around to reading.

HOME TREATMENT

The doctor is attentive when
   His patient gets a sniffle,
But let his child have such a cough
It shakes his little head near off,
   He merely says, "Oh, piffle!"

The doctor is, with pregnancies,
   The sort who tends to worry,
But when his wife begins her pains
All anesthetics he disdains
   And yawns and says, "No hurry."

The moral is as it has been
   Since ages Mesozoic:
If you're a doctor's wife or child
You'd best have only ailments mild
   Or learn to be a stoic.

REALISM

Producers of the "Dr. Kildare" show on TV have hired a physician to coach the actor who fills the part of intern Kildare. —NEWS ITEM

Viewers now are sure to see
Realism on TV,
With interns looking (speaking, too)
The way all real-life interns do.

They'll know the treatment and prognosis
Of tumors, hives, and halitosis.
Their stethoscopes will loosely dangle
Around their necks at just the angle.

And to be really real, on shows
There will be coaches, too, for those
Who play the sick, pain in their glances,
Brought to the set in ambulances.

FRIENDS AND ENEMAS

I hymn the lowly enema,
   A very humble type, O,
Not half so bright or half so keen
   Or sharp as is the hypo.

             The enema's a dullish sort,
               No shiny, dapper dandy.
            And yet it goes where needles can't
               And comes in mighty handy.

No thing of glitter, poised in air,
   No instrument of grace,
There's this about the enema
   At least: it has its place.

DOCTOR, WHAT MAKES YOU SO SHINY?

Since plastic takes the place of wood
   And sometimes even steel,
You can't tell what is plastic now
   By look or even feel.

            The baby has a plastic crib,
               The child has plastic toys,
            And in a plastic coffin one
               Concludes one's earthly joys.

And so, as plastic articles
   Encroach and spread and burgeon,
It frightens me to hear it said,
   "Why, he's a plastic surgeon."

IT TAKES PLUCK

Scientists say that every physical object in the world has a characteristic pitch and vibrates in the same way as a plucked violin string.
—REPORT OF WEISMANN INSTITUTE OF SCIENCE

If this is so, then doctors may,
　　And without hesitation,
Go in for diagnosis by
　　The method of vibration.

Instead of thumping patients, they
　　Will pluck them and then harken,
And if the pitch is slightly off
　　Their worried looks will darken.

But if, plucked like a violin,
　　Somewhere about the middle,
They vibrate with a pitch that's true,
　　They'll say, "Fit as a fiddle."

MURDER FOR LUNCH

Forensic scientists, if you please,
Were eating their lunch (M.D.s, Ph.D.s),
And meanwhile discussing criminalistics
Such as gunshot wounds, powder burns, ballistics.

One sketched on the tablecloth as he said,
"The slug went in here and came out of his head."
Another described, at the very first lull,
How a rapist had bludgeoned his victim's skull.

Two argued, with rival professional pride,
About arsenic versus cyanide. . . .
The talk was lively and gay and bright,
And all had a ravenous appetite.

STUCK WITH IT

Removing adhesive is hazardous work:
Little by little? Or one sudden jerk?
Whichever it is, you may doubt you will win—
Removing adhesive, but leaving the skin.

The patient looks on, quite as anxious, in truth,
As if you're a dentist who's pulling a tooth,
And tenses and stiffens and possibly pales.
(The tensest and stiffest most likely are males.)

Be calm, nonchalant, maybe try a small joke
Or whistle a tune or else proffer a smoke....
Then grab it and yank it from east or from west,
Hope hair's not entangled, and pray for the best.

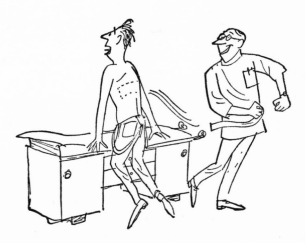

ONE GOOD TOURNIQUET DESERVES ANOTHER

The indiscriminate use of tourniquets, according to a professor at the University of Louisville School of Medicine, can be damaging. —NEWS ITEM

Beware the misused tourniquet
    That stops the blood from flowing.
It should be placed precisely when
    And where by one who's knowing.

A tourniquet should not be used
    Just any time and place.
A pressure dressing may be best,
    For instance on the face.

A patient with a nosebleed, say,
    May wind up quite a wreck
If there's a tourniquet applied,
    And tight, around the neck.

HIGH RATIO

Among the greater metropolitan areas with populations of a million or over, the Boston area has the highest ratio of physicians to population. —NEWS ITEM

Why is it doctors are the thickest
In Boston? Are the people sickest?
If so, and this is rather odd,
Is it from eating beans and cod?

Or do the doctors swarm in legions
Around the proper Back Bay regions
Because they find it elevated
To treat the Harvard-educated?

We do not know the reason, but
To young M.D.s who know what's what
We'd say: Seek out, sir, some metropolis
Where doctors are not quite so popolis.

ELECTRONIC SECRETARY

An electronic secretary enables doctors at the new Palo Alto-Stanford Hospital Center to dictate reports at any hour in the night.   —NEWS ITEM

Punch a button, switch a switch,
And though you have a nervous twitch
And droopy eyelids, reddish eyes,
Your thoughts go down. Then what surprise,

What shock next morning to behold
The sheet of typing, neat and cold,
That says you said the things you said
When you were half (three-quarters) dead.

The push-the-button secretary
Will never leave you, never marry,
And will record, if so you wish,
Each syllable of gibberish.

DOCTOR'S DILEMMA

When going away for a week or a day,
    A curious pickle you land in.
If patients should worsen, some medical person
    Must act as a sort of a stand-in.

The man you select must be keen and correct
    And as good as there is in the town,
Else your patients will swear that you really
                don't care
    And leave you for letting them down.

But here is the trouble that worries you double
    And makes you, with reason, quite grim:
If the substitute lad is too good, it's too bad,
    For your patients will leave you for him!

THE NORMAL MAN

*Psychiatrists picture the "normal man" as a person stable
and contented but a little dull.* —NEWS ITEM

Picture with me, if you can,
The species known as "normal man,"
Not plus or minus, wretch or hero,
But, on the charts, right smack at zero.

He's well adjusted, feels secure,
Has thoughts (when he has thoughts) quite pure.
No eager seeker for success,
He has no ulcers, feels no stress.

Contented as contented cows,
He sleeps at night, by day can drowse.
But is he just a little dull?
Well, conversation's one long lull,

And there are times when, though forgiving,
Friends check his pulse. They doubt he's living.

NORMAL

NEANDERTHAL

FOR OLD GOATS AND OTHERS

Goats suffering from the hereditary neuromuscular disease of myotonia are found to be relieved of their symptoms by depriving them of water. This may yield a clue to the treatment of the comparable disease in humans.

—NEWS ITEM

What works on goats may work on men
  If they can give up water.
They, too, may be all well again
  Though thirsty as a blotter.

But shed no tears of pity, please,
  For those who, with bravura,
Fight manfully the dread disease
  By shunning *aqua pura.*

For though their home's a rural spot
  Or some place that is urban,
They'll have the reason they have sought
  To live on gin or bourbon.

THE AMBULANCE

The ambulance is some machine.
It's rather like a limousine
And also like a station wagon.
It's something, really, you can brag on.

It glides as nicely as you please
And takes the bumps with greatest ease
And has a siren, too, which rocks
The air around for blocks and blocks.

The ambulance is sleek and long,
And sometimes—please don't get me wrong—
When with impatience you are strumming,
It seems as if it's long in coming.

OF AGE

Commonly, physicians, like beer, are best when they are old; and lawyers, like bread, when they are young and new.
—THOMAS FULLER, SEVENTEENTH-CENTURY
ENGLISH CLERGYMAN

The lawyer who's an aging oldie,
Like bread may get all stale and moldy,
Instead, indeed, of growing yummy,
May get to be a little crumby.

The doctor, though, and let us cheer,
Improves with age, like lager beer,
Gets sharp, like Camembert or Cheddar;
Instead of getting worse, gets beddar.

So courage, aging doctor, if'n
Your joints mayhap begin to stiffen.
Remember this, from this here poet:
You're at your best, though you don't know it.

A FEW CRACKS ABOUT BONES

I know a doctor, name of Jones,
Whose specialty is mending bones.
He's glad to help, a skilful schemer,
Whenever someone cracks a femur,
And would, I swear, emplane to Libya
To fix a badly fractured tibia.
He loves his work, he studies late,
"Bones up on bones," he tells his mate,
And gets a certain satisfaction
From seeing limbs held up in traction.
Depend on Jones, in spring or winter,
If leg or arm or hip should splinter.
He's conscientious, as is fitting,
For bone men have to tend their knitting.

REST CURE

Advice that patients love the best
Is this: "You need a nice long rest.
Go hunting, fishing, golfing, please—
Relax, enjoy a life of ease.
Be waited on, stay long in bed,
Of worries and the like be shed.
Go on a tour to distant borders.
Pack up your bag—it's doctor's orders."
And having counseled rest and calm
Beneath, perhaps, some tropic palm,
And having urged a good night's sleep,
Uninterrupted, sound, and deep,
The doctor yawns and rubs his face
And hurries to another case.

PSYCHIATRISTS

Psychiatrists instead of ouches
Hear patients mumbling on their couches.
Instead of soothing sundry pains
They try to calm disordered brains.

They delve into the lurking id
That keeps itself so shyly hid,
But though it might give satisfaction,
Can't tie an ego up in traction.

The catheter they never use,
For it would bring up little news.
The knife they likewise shun, for what
Is there of solid stuff to cut?

And so they grapple and they grope
Without X-ray or fluoroscope
And look inside not head or lung
But books by Adler, Freud, and Jung.

RETIREMENT

The doctor gave his practice up,
    Retired, to read and travel.
No more would he arise at night
    Or hear his patients cavil.

At first he loved his life of ease,
    Was carefree and exultant.
He swore he'd not return to work,
    Not even as consultant.

And did he get his belly full
    Of idleness, and go
Right back to practice, and, indeed,
    Work even harder? No.

FIRST AID, BUT NOT FIRST CLASS

When bandaging a cut or scratch,
I never make a small, neat patch,
But, thanks to looseness in the winding
And slippage in the final binding,
Turn out a thing so large and clumsy
That I'd be laughed at, thought all-thumbsy,
Were I not saved from those who scoff
Because it very soon falls off.

NOTHING BUT THE TOOTH

Talkative factory workers develop carious teeth more readily than do silent ones, according to the British Dental Association.
—NEWS ITEM

Although the evidence is various,
They say that talkers' teeth are carious
More than the teeth of workers who
Just concentrate on what they do.

Could this be caused by more exposure
Of teeth to air? There's no disclosure
As yet, in what we've read, of whether
It's this, or banging more together.

Whatever are the latest guesses
Concerning this, by D.D.S.s,
It's clearly one more reason man
Should keep his mouth shut all he can.

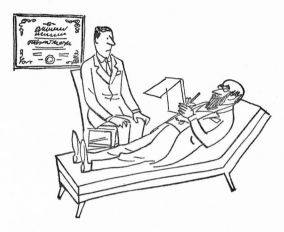

CLINICAL NOTE ON A CLINICAL NOTE

Psychiatry has been called the "science of sympathy."
—POSTGRADUATE MEDICINE

When I consider all the yak
He has to hear, and not talk back,
The problems he must grasp, though spiky,
Tossed at him by a spiteful psyche,

When I consider, too, how much
He deals with what he cannot touch
Or see, and how he's lost amid
The realm of ego and of id,

When I consider he's the butt
Of feeble joke and unkind cut
From people such as I, I see
Who ought to have the sympathy.

CRITERIA FOR NURSES

Doctors like their nurses neat,
With well-washed hands and quiet feet.
They like them, if not quite omniscient,
At least well-trained, alert, proficient.

Unflustered, cool, and always ready.
Doctors like their nurses steady,
They like them punctual and tireless,
Good-humored, cheerful, ever ireless.

But doctors' wives, as is their way,
At home, imagining, all day,
Hope just one thing, while dusting, cooking:
Those nurses aren't too darned good-looking!

YOUNG DOCTORS

Young doctors, when they're starting out,
  May know the heart and lung,
May know diseases, cause and cure,
  But simply look too young.

They grow mustaches, even beards,
  They puff upon a pipe.
They wrinkle brows, they stoop a bit
  To seem an older type.

Young doctors are afflicted with
  An ailment they despair of.
Like some conditions, theirs is one
  That time alone takes care of.

WRITE AND WRONG

Things are often said quite biting
About a doctor's way of writing—
The hieroglyphic tracks of hen
That burgeon underneath his pen,
The hand that no one but his wife or
A keen-eyed druggist can decipher.

But though the doctor's script draws curses,
It's nothing, sometimes, to his nurse's—
A penmanship so full of scribbles
And blots and blurs and inky dribbles
That records get to be so heinous
You can't tell "sinus," oft, from "anus."

KEEPING INFORMED

One thing that is really not difficult, friends,
Is keeping abreast of new medical trends,
New treatments, new gadgets, new antibiotics,
New cures for the ailing, including neurotics.

And if you don't learn from attending a meeting
Or glancing at journals, though glances be fleeting,
Or talking with colleagues, you'll not be without it,
For surely your patient has read all about it.

AFTER THE BRAWL WAS OVER

It took 40 trucks to cart away the debris after the AMA
convention in Chicago. —MEDICAL NEWS

Forty trucks to carry off,
  With not a little trouble,
The empty bottles, paper cups,
  The well-assorted rubble,

The read and unread documents
  (The latter the majority),
The hats, the shirts, the worn-out shoes,
  The badges of authority.

However, but for all the tons
  Of stuff lugged off to sample,
In bulging bags, a thousand trucks
  Would hardly have been ample.

THE EYES HAVE IT

Research reported at an optometrists' meeting in Milwaukee indicates that more than 65 per cent of the people who suffer from chronic headaches have one eye located higher in their heads than the other. —NEWS ITEM

Next time a patient has a headache,
A splitting, throbbing, piercing dread ache,
Don't worry about spine or brain
Or give a pill to kill the pain.
Don't think of things like hypertension
Or other ills that one might mention,
Just look the patient in the eye.
Is one an inch or so too high?
And has the patient thus no chance
To look about with even glance?
It might be this—a low or highness,
A kind of ocular awryness—
That causes headaches. If it does,
Don't mention it, my friend, because
To know one's eyes aren't on the level
Would make one's head ache like the devil!

TURNOVER

The old nurse knew where things were kept,
    Could find them very quickly.
The new nurse, such a helpless thing,
    Just stands there smiling sickly.

The old nurse knew the patients' names
    As well as their addresses.
The new nurse hardly knows her own
    And makes some ghastly guesses.

How strange to think it won't be long
    (Sad prospect, but a true one)
Till this nurse is the old nurse and
    You lose her for a new one.

HAIR-RAISING STORY

According to the AMA, the first recorded prescription for a hair grower was made up for the Egyptian Queen Ses, mother of King Teta, in 3400 B.C. —NEWS ITEM

We wonder, was the lady called
Queen Ses the person who was bald,
Or did she have the stuff, when done,
Delivered to her thin-haired son?

Or, since it is the female who
Transmits the tendency, it's true,
Perhaps (to say it I am loath)
Not one was short of hair, but both.

This much, however, we can guess
Regarding Teta and Queen Ses:
Whoever, in that ancient day,
Was bald, most likely stayed that way.

IT COULD BE WORSE

It seems that people who are able
To read a book can't read a label,
Can't comprehend, when feeling aily,
How many times is "three times daily,"
Can't tell if it's a large or wee spoon
When very plainly it says "teaspoon,"
Can't figure out the go-ahead time
When it is written, "Take at bedtime."

The way they phone to ask repeatedly
(Some doctors answer rather heatedly)
To have the label's words translated
And very simple terms equated,
We're only glad that they're not needing
Such help as this with *all* their reading.

ONE WHO NEEDS NO INTRODUCTION

Dr. X,
  A splendid surgeon,
At banquets speaks
  Without much urgin'.

> He takes the floor,
>   Alas, alack,
> And some hours later
>   Gives it back.

> He clears his throat,
>   He sips his drink,
> He hems and haws
>   And stops to think.

> In surgery
>   He's sure and swift,
> His way with scalpels
>   Is a gift.

He can trepan
  The thickest skull. . . .
His knife is sharp—
  His tongue is dull.

ROOM SERVICE

Put your patient in a ward,
   A biggish room, and sunny.
Put him in with three or four
   To save his hard-earned money.
And what will happen? He will howl
   He doesn't care for pelf,
And though he has to borrow cash
   He *must* be by himself!

Put your patient, who can well
   Afford the very best,
Into a splendid single room
   For quiet and for rest.
And what will happen? He will scream
   And carry on and moan.
He needs some company, he does—
   He *will* not be alone!

DOCTOR'S DAY OFF

Some doctors on their day off like
   To golf, the day permitting.
Some like to walk, and some prefer
   Just sitting.

Some doctors like to read the book
   They've never quite had time for,
Or watch TV and drink the drink
   They've lime for. . . .

But all who know the sound of phone
   And doorbell on the day off
Agree the safest place to be
   Is way off.

TO HELL WITH HIPPOCRATES!

GUEST CONSULTANT

At parties he's in much demand:
The hostess seats him close at hand
And all the guests are pleased as Punch
He came to dinner or to lunch.

And is he, then, a beau, a wit,
By whom the ladies like to sit?
Oh, no—each hopes the guest M.D.
Will diagnose her ailments free.

THE GYNECOLOGIST

The gynecologist knows best
  Just what makes women tick.
He tends them very tenderly
  Whenever they are sick.

He knows their troubles, large or small,
  Can diagnose and cure,
And, very seldom at a loss,
  He's confident and sure.

What ails a woman when she's ill?
  It's likely he can tell.
And yet I swear not even he
  Can cope with one who's well.

STOP STICKING OUT YOUR TONGUE
AT THE DOCTOR

*A British doctor says the practice of looking at patients'
tongues is a complete waste of time. A furry tongue means
a patient has a furry tongue and nothing else.*

—NEWS ITEM

Henceforth a patient need not worry
About a tongue that's white and furry.
It merely means, in old and young,
The patient has a furry tongue.
A helpful principle is this.
How can the diagnosis miss?
It's something all can understand:

A swollen gland's a swollen gland,
An ache's an ache, a throb's a throb,
A lump's a lump, a knob's a knob,
A patient with a bad relapse
Has, well, a bad relapse perhaps.
But (back to tongues) if this is so,
Now patients who have tongues to show
May stick them out at whom they please,
Except, quite possibly, M.D.s.

FAT CHANCE

*There is a possibility that obesity is caused by a disorder
of the hypothalamus.* —NEWS ITEM

Let's say you have a patient who
Eats more than anyone, or two,
And of the many things she eats
Most loves to gorge on starches, sweets.

Now you could tell her she is lacking
In self-control, and have my backing,
Or make her switch, if all else fails,
To biting on her fingernails.

Or you could say, "Now don't you fuss,
It's naughty hypothalamus,
No fault of yours." She'd love you dearly,
And get to weigh a ton, or nearly.

GRAFT

The successful use of calf bone for grafts in human beings was reported at the meeting of the American College of Surgeons. —NEWS ITEM

How eagerly I wait the day
   (I laugh a nervous laugh)
When someone's leg is grafted and
   His calf is really calf.

      Then, even though the flesh itself
        Is human, with some pride
      He'll show his lower leg and say,
         "My calf is calf inside."

            There is a risk, however, here,
              And I can tell you how:
            A calf won't stay a calf, it will
              In time become a cow.

THE G.P.

The general practitioner
   I hail, salute, and sing,
The man who really needs to know
   A bit of everything.

While others stick to nose and throat
   Or allergies or ears
Or bones or skin or brain or glands
   Or lungs or psychic fears,

He has to know the whole shebang,
   From soles of feet to scalp,
For there are times he can't look blank
   And helplessly cry, "Halp!"

The specialists keep shorter hours
   And get a higher fee,
But he outranks them all, for he's
   A general, you see.

QUICK SERVICE

Patients are impatient folk
Who will not wait to hear a joke
Or even pass the time of day,
But want their health back, right away.

They hate to sit there one full minute,
Mouth shut (thermometer jammed in it).
They can't bear waiting, not a bit,
For wounds to heal and bones to knit.

They want to be all well at once.
If you can't do it, you're a dunce.
And though they summon a physician,
They really need a good magician.

THE HAPPY WORRIER

Experiments at Walter Reed Army Hospital indicate that ulcers are found more in people who worry off and on than in those who worry steadily. —NEWS ITEM

Consider those unhappy men
Who only worry now and then,
Who grow all tense and then relax,
Which makes their ulcers run in packs.

More fortunate the steady worriers,
The always pressing, straining hurriers,
Who not one moment cease to frown,
And thereby keep their ulcers down.

Yes, constant worry does the trick.
It's sure to help the ulcer-sick,
Who'll lose their ulcers, in the shakedown,
And merely have a nervous breakdown.

STOCKING UP

Why does the doctor's helpmate tag
   Along at each convention?
The reason's one, all said and done,
   We really hate to mention.

Is it to shield his roving eye
   And check his clumsy passes?
Or maybe frown his quaffing down
   To somewhat fewer glasses?

Good reasons, these, to go along,
   And in themselves quite ample,
But mostly she's on hand to seize
   Free sample after sample.

NO-NONSENSE M.D.

Beat the drum and wave the banner.
Applaud this doctor's bedside manner.
He doesn't butter up old ladies;
If they're not sick, he gives them Hades.
He doesn't cluck his tongue impressively,
He doesn't ever laugh excessively.
His brow's not wrinkled like Ed Murrow,
He's brisk and businesslike, but thorough.
He wastes no time in idle chatter,
But when he's found out what's the matter
He does what's called for, all that's needed,
And then departs. Not that he's speeded
By patients waiting for his call—
His practice is, it seems, quite small.

IN THE BAG

The little black bag is carefully packed
   With each sort of pill and potion.
The boxes and bottles are wedged or stacked
   With skill and with loving devotion.

There are items like bandage and cotton and tape
   And a pack of depressors right near 'em.
There are gadgets to pull with, to cut with, or scrape,
   And an ample assortment of serum.

The little black bag is now heavy with gear,
   And its owner is patientward speeded.
And all that is lacking is this, I fear:
   Whatever is vitally needed.

HOSPITAL VISITORS

They come at unexpected hours
   With grim, depressing faces
And large bouquets of smelly flowers
   For overflowing vases.

They come alone, by twos, by threes,
   These friends and close relations,
And talk, with germy cough and sneeze,
   About their operations.

And when the patient nears relapse,
   The nurse takes no more chances.
She clears the room. Does she, perhaps,
   Get thanks? No, ugly glances.

IDEAL PATIENT

The perfect patient let us praise:
He's never sick on Saturdays,
In fact this wondrous, welcome wight
Is also never sick at night.
In waiting rooms he does not burn
But gladly sits and waits his turn,
And even, I have heard it said,
Begs others, "Please, go on ahead."
He takes advice, he does as told,
He has a heart of solid gold.
He pays his bills, without a fail,
In cash, or by the same day's mail.
He has but one small fault I'd list:
He doesn't (what a shame!) exist.

115

PREPARATION FOR PAIN

In many operating rooms, just before anesthesia hits the patient such calming music as "Clair de Lune," "Moonlight Sonata," and "Forest Murmurs" is used to drown out ominous sounds.
                                                            —NEWS ITEM

Soft strains of music drown the clatter
Of scalpels being rearranged
And calm the heart's quick pitter-patter.
(The records are, like dressings, changed.)

Inaudible the sterilizer,
The hiss of gas, the drip of water.
The patient hears (he's none the wiser
About some things) "Moonlight Sonata."

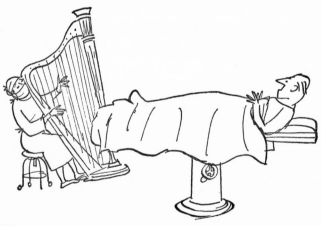

Until the anesthetics nix him
He may not feel quite up to par,
But "Forest Murmurs" ought to fix him,
Or "Clair de Lune" or "Evening Star."

Unless, of course, his taste should run to
Bartok, Stravinsky, and Ravel—
When, having thus a while been done to,
He'll groan, "Come, cut me. Might as well."

MEMORY AID

"Doctor," she says, "I have written a list
    Of my symptoms, for fear I'd forget them.
They're here in my bag, if I only can find
    The paper on which I have set them.

"Yes, here they are, doctor; I have here the list
    Of the things that I've carefully noted:
A pain that begins in the small of my back
    And my being so terribly bloated,

"And a dozen loin chops and it hurts me to
                breathe
    And a couple of pounds of tomatoes
And a rash on my chest and a small piece of
                cheese
    And chills and a sack of potatoes."

SURE SIGN

It's not by the lack of a fever you tell
That a patient is mending and soon will be well.
It's not by the fact that his tongue is uncoated,
His color is good, and his stomach's not bloated,
No, not by the fact that his pains now are less
That you know that he's starting to convalesce.
It's not that his pulse rate is steady and slow
And his blood pressure's down, now, three days in a
    row. . . .
Here's a sign of recovery, big as a bus:
He has given up praying, and started to cuss.

DEPRECIATION

Come income tax time, a doctor
   Must rally his faltering senses
And gather his files all about him
   And search through his stubs for expenses.

Then, worn from the calls he's been making
   At three and at four in the morning,
And patients with ailments that baffle
   And births without adequate warning,

He thinks, as he peers at the mirror
   That faces him over the shelf,
That they ought to allow a deduction
   For wear and for tear on himself.

CURRENT PRACTICE

With wires to the brain and with wires to the heart,
With gadgets that test and with gauges that chart,

With knives that plug in, either AC or DC,
For cutting through surfaces, smooth ones or creasy,

With every new sort of electric computer,
To check on the positive, negative, neuter,

With rays of both X and of infrared kinds
For treating the outsides and insides and minds,

With all these devices, the modern physician
Needs nothing so much as a good electrician.

STEADY DOES IT

The doctor's working on a case,
  One must admire his poise.
He works with dedicated zeal,
  It's work that he enjoys.

The doctor's working on a case,
  As anyone may see.
He has a certain touch, a flair,
  And great capacity.

He's systematic, thorough, sure,
  Experienced and deft.
The doctor's working on a case—
  There's just one bottle left.

IT SAYS HERE

We have a suggestion regarding the cure
That, although still untested on humans, is sure,
The one that your patients request—yes, demand,
With the article telling about it in hand.

It is, says the piece in the magazine
In which it appeared and by millions was seen,
All ready to go (and it's perfectly true
That so far it has worked on a hamster or two) .

We have a suggestion to remedy this:
To make very certain, not be hit-or-miss,
Let's test it on people, and, though a small particle,
Try it first on the fellow who wrote the darned article.

BELL HOP

The telephone's a splendid thing
   Which, thanks to Mr. Bell,
Permits a patient to acquire
   Advice when not too well.

The telephone, both day and night,
   Is always close at hand.
The doctor may be fast asleep,
   But he will understand.

The telephone's no great expense,
   It's easily installed.
And Mr. Bell, the lucky guy,
   Is where he's never called.

TAKE A SQUINT

See the little spots and dots
   Beneath the microscope.
See the bars and tiny rings,
See all shapes and kinds of things.
   Doctor, what's the dope?

Look low and high with practiced eye,
   Be thorough, be punctilious.
Are those malignant organisms
You see beneath those potent prisms,
   Or, doctor, are you bilious?

FATHER AND SON

It isn't strange at all if one
Should earnestly advise his son
Against a medical career
And tell him of the year on year
Of painful toil, incessant study,
And gruesome sights, macabre and bloody,
And time of little earning when
One sees the rise of other men,
And after this, long hours to keep,
And bone-tired days and broken sleep.
Nor is it strange at all if one,
When everything is said and done,
Should dream a bit and see the lad
Some day in practice with his Dad.

EXPERT'S ADVICE

Some people travel miles to see
A highly trained, well-known M.D.,
A specialist whose reputation
Is heralded throughout the nation.

They seek advice about their ill
From someone who has special skill,
And listen to his words because
He ought to know if any does.

And having journeyed, man or maid,
So very far, and having paid
For this advice a wad of dough,
Do you suppose they take it?
No!

NEXT STEP AFTER SOCIALIZED MEDICINE

When patients wonder if it's gas
    Or ulcers or cirrhosis,
They'll put a nickel in the slot
    And get a diagnosis.

They'll slip a printed time card in
    And press a little button,
And out will come the cure, and it
    Will cost them next to nutton.

But oh, the woe, the gnashing teeth,
    From border unto border,
When on the medical machine
    The sign says, "Out of Order."

NURSE, HAND ME MY OIL CAN

Will automation do away
With doctors, also, some fine day?
Will patients then, when they are ill,
Just press a button for a pill?

Will metal monsters cut the skin
With scalpels, probe around within,
And having done what's needed, then
Stitch up the patient once again?

If things should come to such a pass,
With doctors mostly steel or brass,
There should be little cause for rue,
For patients will be robots too.

ABOUT THE AUTHOR AND
THE ILLUSTRATOR

RICHARD ARMOUR, a graduate of Pomona College and a Ph.D. from Harvard University, has been a member of the faculty of such institutions as Wells College, the University of Texas, Northwestern University, the University of Hawaii, the University of Freiburg, and the Claremont Graduate School, and has held teaching and research fellowships from Harvard University, the Carnegie Corporation, and the Fund for the Advancement of Education. He is now Dean of the Faculty and Professor of English at Scripps College, in Claremont, California. He is best known, however, as the contributor of several thousand pieces of frolicsome verse and prose to more than one hundred magazines in the United States and England, and as the author of a long list of bestselling books of humor and satire, including *It All Started with Columbus, It All Started with Eve, Twisted Tales from Shakespeare, Drug Store Days, Golf Is a Four-Letter Word,* and *Armour's Almanac.* This is his twenty-third book.

LEO HERSHFIELD, one of America's most popular and prolific illustrators, has brightened the pages of *The Saturday Evening Post, Changing Times,* and many other magazines. He has illustrated the books of several well-known authors, and this is his fifth with Richard Armour. A resident of Bradenton, Florida, he manages to keep healthy by spending as much time as he can on his sailboat.